THE
Great
Apes

BY GEOFFREY C. SAIGN

A First Book

FRANKLIN WATTS   A Division of Grolier Publishing

New York • London • Hong Kong • Sydney • Danbury, Connecticut

For Ken, Joseph, Bobby, and Tommy

Photographs ©: Ellis Nature Photography: cover bottom right, cover bottom left, 12, 14, 17, 18, 20 (Gerry Ellis), 50 (Konrad Wothe); The Gorilla Foundation/Dr. Ronald H. Cohn: 27; National Geographic Society: 37 (Jane Goodall), 54 (Baron Hugo Van Lawick), 33 (Kenneth Love), 4, 6, 48, 56 (Michael K. Nichols), 22 (Peter G. Velt), 58; Photo Researchers: 53 (Tim Davis), 34 (Nigel J. Dennis), cover top (Kenneth W. Fink), 10 (David Gifford/SPL), 28, 31, 45, 46, 51 (Renee Lynn), 25, 40 (Tom McHugh), 39 (R. Van Nostrand); Visuals Unlimited: 42 (Leonard Lee Rue III), cover back, 23 (Joe McDonald).

Library of Congress Cataloging-in-Publication Data

Saign, Geoffrey 1955–
        The great apes / Geoffrey C. Saign
        p.   cm. — (A First book)
        Includes bibliographical references and index.
        Summary: Describes and compares the four great apes: chimpanzees, bonobos, orangutans, and gorillas through a discussion of their physical, intellectual, emotional, and social characteristics.
        ISBN 0-531-20361-1 (lib. bdg.)   0-531-15902-7 (pbk.)
        1. Apes—Juvenile literature.   [1. Apes.]   I. Title.   II. Series.
        QL737.P96S23   1998
        599.88—dc21   97-1189

                                                                    CIP
                                                                    AC

contents

Great apes are the closest living relatives to humans.

introduction

On August 16, 1996, a 3-year-old boy was watching the gorillas at the Brookfield Zoo near Chicago, Illinois. In his excitement, he began climbing the fence. When he reached the top, he lost his balance and fell 18 feet (5.5 m) into the gorilla pit!

Everyone was terrified as Binti-Jua, a female lowland gorilla, moved toward the boy. At the time, Binti-Jua was carrying her own baby against her chest. When she reached the boy, she gently picked him up and carried him to the cage entrance, where zookeepers were anxiously watching. A gorilla had saved the boy!

Movies such as *King Kong* portray gorillas as fierce, frightening animals. And sometimes great apes do fight. Occasionally, they even kill each other. But most of the time, they are very gentle and shy.

Great apes are truly great because they are almost as intelligent as humans. They can solve problems and use tools. They show a whole range of emotions and have many social relationships.

They are our closest living relatives in the world. The common ancestor we share with the great apes isn't alive today. It lived about 5 million to 7 million years ago. That may seem like a long time ago, but compared to all the time that has passed since Earth was created, it's like the blink of an eye.

Chimpanzees are primates—so are lemurs, bush babies, tarsiers, marmosets, monkeys, gibbons, apes, orangutans, bonobos, and humans.

1
What Is a Great Ape?

All great apes are *primates*. You are a primate, too. Primates are animals with forward-facing eyes, *stereoscopic* (3-D) and color vision, and *prehensile* hands that can grip and hold things because the thumbs are opposite the fingers. Primates are intelligent animals with large, well-developed brains.

There are about 230 *species* of primates in the world. Scientists divide them into two groups: prosimians and anthropoids. The prosimians include the more primitive lemurs, bush babies, and tarsiers. The anthropoids include marmosets, tamarins, monkeys, lesser apes (gibbons), great apes, and humans. One of the major differences between apes

7

COMPARING THE GREAT APES

GREAT APE	BODY SIZE	HABITAT/BEHAVIOR
GORILLAS	Largest great ape/ largest primate; Males: 400 pounds (180 kg), up to 6 feet (1.8 m) when standing; Females: 200 pounds (90 kg), up to 5 feet (1.5 m) when standing	Live in troops of 5 to 20 members with a leader; young may stay with mother for 3 to 4 years and stay near her for up to 10 years; eat plants and, occasionally, insects; spend most of their time on the ground; display many emotions; can solve problems and learn *sign language*; may live more than 50 years
COMMON CHIMPANZEES	Males: 115 pounds (52 kg), up to 4.5 feet (1.4 m) when standing; Females: 90 pounds (40.5 kg), up to 4 feet (1.2 m) when standing	Live in communities of 15 to 80 members with a male leader; young may stay near mother for their entire lives; eat plants, some insects, and mammals; hunt and fight enemies in groups; live in trees and on the ground; display many emotions; can solve problems and learn sign language; make and use tools; may live more than 50 years
BONOBOS (Pygmy chimpanzee)	Smallest great ape; Males: 100 pounds (45 kg), up to 3.3 feet (1 m) when standing; Females: 75 pounds (34 kg), up to 3.3 feet (1 m) when standing	Live in close-knit communities in which females play a central role; young may stay near mother all their lives; eat plants, some insects, and, occasionally, mammals; spend more time in trees than common chimpanzees; more peaceful than common chimpanzees; display many emotions; can solve problems and learn sign language; use tools less frequently than common chimpanzees; may live more than 50 years
ORANGUTANS	Largest tree-dwelling animal; Males: 200 pounds (90 kg), up to 4.5 feet (1.4 m) long; Females: 110 pounds (50 kg), up 3.5 feet (1.1 m) long	Adult males are solitary and sometimes *nomadic*; young stay with mother 4 to 5 years; eat plants, some insects, eggs, honey, and, occasionally, mammals; display many emotions; can solve problems and learn sign language; some make and use tools; live 50 to 60 years

8

and most other primates is that apes do not have tails.

There are four types of great apes: gorillas, chimpanzees, bonobos, and orangutans. The table on page 8 describes their major characteristics.

◈◦◈ FROM APE TO HUMAN ◈◦◈

About 65 million years ago, a group of small, ground-dwelling mammals began living in trees—these were the ancestors of today's primates. Then, about 25 million years ago, some of these tree dwellers left the trees to live on the ground again. They became the ancestors of today's great apes.

About 5 million years ago, one group of great apes began to change and develop. Eventually, the descendants of this group *evolved* into early humans. All humans and their direct ancestors belong to a group called the *hominids*. Many scientists believe the African great apes are so similar to humans that they should also be considered hominids. In other words, humans are really just specialized great apes.

How do we know that humans and great apes are so closely related? To answer this question, let's try thinking about it in a slightly different way. How do people know that you are related to your parents or your brother or sister? You may have the same straight or curly hair as close family members. Your eyes may be the same color as theirs. Or you may have the same

Great apes and humans share a common ancestor. Early humans evolved from an apelike ancestor about 5 million years ago.

type of nose or mouth or ears. In other words, you have more ***traits*** in common with close relatives than with other people.

In the same way, scientists know that humans have much more in common with great apes than with mice or salamanders or mosquitoes. In fact, chimpanzees are more closely related to humans than they are to gorillas! The table below lists the ways in which great apes resemble humans.

So how do great apes differ from humans? Great apes have arms longer than their legs. They also have bigger jawbones, and usually walk on all fours. Humans are the only primates that stand upright and walk on

SIMILARITIES BETWEEN GREAT APES AND HUMANS

TRAIT	GREAT APES	HUMANS
LARGE, COMPLEX BRAINS	✸	✸
FORWARD-FACING EYES	✸	✸
3-D AND COLOR VISION	✸	✸
PREHENSILE HANDS	✸	✸
PREHENSILE FEET	✸	
NO TAIL	✸	✸
THIRTY-TWO TEETH	✸	✸
ARMS LONGER THAN LEGS	✸	
ALWAYS WALK ON TWO LEGS		✸
LIVE IN TREES	✸	
USE TOOLS	✸	✸
VERY INTELLIGENT	✸	✸
WIDE RANGE OF EMOTIONS	✸	✸

This orangutan and all other great apes have prehensile feet and hands, so they can grip tree branches and other objects.

two legs all the time. Because we walk upright, our feet are arched. Great apes have flat, prehensile feet with big toes that are opposable—like thumbs—so their feet can grip tree branches just like their hands.

If Your Thumbs Weren't Opposable

Only primates have prehensile hands with opposable thumbs. To get an idea of what life would be like if we didn't have hands with thumbs opposite our fingers, try the following activity.

Wrap masking tape around one hand so that your thumb is pressed against your pointer finger. Now try to pick up a penny or an orange. It's pretty difficult, isn't it? Before you remove the tape, try to drink a glass of water, write a short note, peel a banana, or use scissors. Aren't you glad you have opposable thumbs? Most animals aren't so lucky.

Gorillas begin feeding in the early morning. Male gorillas often stand guard while females and youngsters eat.

2
Gorillas

It is early morning in the tropical *rain forest*. A small group of gorillas is enjoying breakfast. A *silverback,* the troop's dominant male, is standing guard nearby. The moment the silverback spots a leopard quietly stalking one of the gorilla babies, it rears up on its hind legs and beats its chest with its open hands, making a loud threatening sound. The big gorilla then hoots and roars as it charges the leopard on all fours. The startled leopard races away—it is no match for a gorilla! The silverback quickly calms down and returns to his troop.

A leopard may occasionally catch a baby gorilla or kill a sick adult, but healthy adult gorillas have no real enemies in the jungle—except humans. No jungle animal can stand up to the strength of a male silverback.

⬦ A GORILLA'S DAY ⬦

All wild gorillas live in Africa. Lowland gorillas live in very hot, dense rain forests in East and West Africa. Mountain gorillas live in the cooler, dense Virunga Mountain rain forests of Zaire, Rwanda, and Uganda. To see mountain gorillas in their natural **habitat,** you'd have to climb to an **altitude** of 5,000 to 12,000 feet (1,524 to 3,658 m).

Gorillas like thick rain forests because they are plant eaters. Their favorite foods include bamboo, wild celery, and blackberries. Each day, they spend several hours wandering through the lush forest in search of food. While mountain gorillas often travel only a few hundred yards each day in search of food, lowland gorillas must go much farther. A large adult gorilla eats 45 to 65 pounds (20 to 29 kg) of leaves, branches, fruit, roots, and stems every day.

Gorillas use their long fingers to peel away the hard outer parts of plant stems, so they can eat the juicy inner parts. And just like some people, gorillas like to hum, grunt, or smack their lips when eating.

Gorillas love to bask in the sun. When it rains, most gorillas sit with their knees pulled close to their chests or wait under a tree until the storm is over. Some

Gorillas use their flexible fingers to peel off the hard outer parts of plants so they can eat the soft, juicy inner parts.

lowland gorillas don't mind getting wet, however. Recently, scientists working in the Republic of Congo saw a lowland gorilla wading up to its chest in a pond.

Every day and night, gorillas make nests to nap and sleep in. They never use the same nest twice.

18

Adult female gorillas sometimes climb trees to rest, eat, or get away from *predators* or other gorillas. Adult male gorillas weigh more than females, so they spend most of their time on the ground. Baby gorillas spend a lot of time in trees and like to swing from tree branch to tree branch.

How are gorillas like birds? They both sleep in nests! But, unlike a bird's nest, a gorilla's nest takes only a few minutes to build. It's just a pile of broken branches and leaves. Adult males build nests on the ground, while young gorillas and females often build nests in trees. Baby gorillas sleep in their mother's nest until they are about 4 years old. Gorillas are constantly on the move—they never use the same nest twice.

❖ THE GORILLA BODY ❖

There is only one species of gorilla, but scientists have divided that species into three *subspecies*: the mountain gorilla, the eastern lowland gorilla, and the western lowland gorilla. Although all three types of gorillas look very similar, a careful observer can see some differences. Because mountain gorillas live in a cooler habitat, they have long, thick hair to keep them warm. Their hair is also darker than that of lowland gorillas. Eastern lowland gorillas are larger than other gorillas.

A male gorilla matures when it is 10 to 13 years old. At this age, each male grows a thick crown of hair on its head, the hair on its chest falls out, and the hair on its back turns silver-gray. That is why the dominant male of a *troop* is called a silverback. Younger male gorillas are called blackbacks.

Adult male gorillas have silver hair on their backs and are called silverbacks. A silverback is the leader of its gorilla troop.

Male gorillas have wide, massive chests, and powerful shoulders, necks, and backs. They also have potbellies. In human males, potbellies are considered unhealthy, but they are normal in gorillas. Female gorillas mature when they are about 8 years old. All females and babies have black hair.

Gorillas are the largest type of primate. An adult male may weigh more than 400 pounds (180 kg). A silverback standing on two legs may be up to 6 feet (1.8 m) tall. Female gorillas are smaller and weigh half as much as silverbacks—about 200 pounds (90 kg).

Gorillas walk on all fours, resting on their front knuckles. In this position, they usually stand 3 to 4 feet (1 to 1.2 m) high. Their outstretched arms may span more than 8 feet (2.4 m). They can stand upright on their hind legs for only a few minutes at a time. They move 3 to 4 miles (4.8 to 6.4 km) per hour.

Gorillas have huge heads, large jaw muscles, and big sharp teeth. Scientists believe that gorillas' sight, hearing, and sense of smell are like those of humans. Because their vocal cords are different from ours, they can't speak like we do. They can, however, make several dozen sounds. They bark when they are curious, roar when they are angry, hoot when they are alarmed, grunt to let others know where they are, and even mumble softly and belch when they feel good. Most of the time, however, gorillas are quiet animals.

A gorilla troop is like a big family. Each troop has one silverback, several females, some young males, and babies.

❖❖ GORILLA TROOPS ❖❖

A troop of gorillas usually consists of two to thirty members. Each troop is like a big family. It includes one silverback and several females as well as young males and babies. The silverback is the leader and guardian of a gorilla troop. The silverback will give its life to protect its troop. The silverback decides when to stay in an area and when to leave. No one in the troop argues with the boss. The silverback also settles conflicts. If two gorillas fight over food, the silverback only has to stare at them to make them stop fighting.

When silverbacks protect their troop, or fight another male, they may beat their chests or grunt and yell.

Silverbacks are *polygamous*—they mate with several females. Only the troop's silverback mates with the females, so all the babies in the troop are his *offspring*. When younger males and females mature, they may leave the troop to find their own mates. Sometimes one silverback will fight another for control of a troop.

When silverbacks fight, they first stare at each other, then they beat their chests, grunt, yell, and break branches off trees. Only occasionally do they actually hit or bite each other. When one gorilla feels it has lost the fight, it leaves the area or just stares at the ground. In this way, one silverback tells another that it is giving up. When a silverback seizes control of a new troop or takes a new female into the troop, it often kills the babies of other males.

Gorilla troops live a relaxed life. They spend their mornings and afternoons finding and eating their favorite foods. In between, the adults nap in nests, while the young gorillas wrestle and play. The gorillas also spend time grooming each other—picking ticks and dirt out of their fur. A gorilla's day is usually very peaceful.

⬦ GORILLA BABIES ⬦

Females are pregnant for 8½ months and usually give birth to only one 5-pound (2.3-kg) baby every 3 to 4 years. Occasionally, gorillas have twins. Like a human

Baby gorillas are born helpless, like human babies. They cling to their mother's back until they can walk.

baby, a gorilla baby is born helpless. It clings piggyback to its protective mother. Gorilla babies grow teeth in about 6 weeks. At 2½ months of age, they start to eat plants. After 4 months, the babies can walk on all fours. By the time they are 6 months old, they weigh about 15 pounds (7 kg).

Baby gorillas love to play! They tickle each other and wrestle. They even play follow-the-leader and tag. All the gorillas in a troop, including the silverbacks, play gently with the babies. A baby gorilla may stay with its mother for 3 to 4 years, and may stay near its mother for up to 10 years.

◈ SHOWING HOW THEY FEEL ◈

Gorillas are gentle and shy—and very smart. A 15-year-old lowland gorilla named Koko has been learning sign language for 14 years. She now knows more than 500 signs and can talk with people who know sign language. She even used sign language to ask for a pet kitten, which she named All Ball.

By studying Koko and wild gorillas, people have learned that these animals are very intelligent and show many of the same emotions as humans. They can feel scared, happy, excited, nervous, sad, playful, lonely, hurt, angry, upset, curious, protective, or loving. Just like human infants, baby gorillas need a lot of love and nurturing to grow into healthy adults. If females do not receive a lot of love and nurturing as babies, they do not know how to be good mothers.

Koko, a lowland gorilla, gently touches her pet kitten for the first time. Koko asked for a pet kitten and named it All Ball.

Chimpanzees are skilled tool users. This one is using a straight
stick to "fish" for termites in a log.

3

Chimpanzees and Bonobos

If you were hungry for termites, what would you do? Watch a chimpanzee! First, a chimpanzee carefully finds a long blade of grass or grabs a slender tree branch and breaks off its leaves. Then it slides the grass or stick into the hole of a termite nest. The termites think their nest is being invaded and bite the stick with their pincers. The chimpanzee pulls the stick out of the nest and quickly eats the termites stuck to it— yummy! Scientists have found that it takes a great deal of practice to do this as well as a chimpanzee.

Chimpanzees are like humans in the way they use tools and hunt in groups. They also look and behave more like humans than any other animal does.

❖❖ USING TOOLS AND COMMON SENSE ❖❖

Chimpanzees use many tools. They use long blades of grass or sticks to catch ants and termites. They use carefully selected rocks to break open nuts. They use leaves to clean their sticky hands after a meal of fruit, to clean their fur, and to absorb water from places they can't reach with their mouths. They even scare other animals by throwing rocks and shaking sticks at them!

Chimpanzees use reason—they solve problems by thinking about them. For example, chimpanzees in captivity will pile up boxes if they want to reach something high—just like a human might use a ladder.

A chimpanzee named Washoe was taught sign language. She has learned more than 300 signs and even made up some signs of her own. Washoe's son learned 50 of these signs from his mother without ever seeing humans do them. Other chimpanzees have learned to use symbols on a computer keyboard to ask questions and request food. Wild chimpanzees learn things very quickly from one another.

❖❖ CHIMPANZEES EXPRESS THEMSELVES ❖❖

Like gorillas, chimpanzees show almost as many emotions as humans. They can be sad, angry, disappointed, impatient, frustrated, happy, loving, or protective. They even have a sense of humor; they love to tickle each

Touch is very important for humans and for chimpanzees. It helps them to feel calm, safe, and loved.

other and laugh! They can also appreciate beauty in nature. Researchers have seen them watch a breathtaking sunset for up to 15 minutes!

Chimpanzees communicate their feelings in a variety of ways. They can make about thirty-five sounds, and are often quite noisy. They also communicate with **body language**—they use facial expressions and body movements to show when they are happy, angry, excited, or sad. When a chimpanzee seems to be smiling, it is actually frightened or excited.

Chimpanzees also communicate by touching. They greet each other with kisses and hugs, hold hands, pat each other on the back, and groom one another. Touching helps them feel safe, secure, and happy.

How strong are a chimpanzee's feelings? If a young chimpanzee's mother dies, it sometimes feel so sad that it refuses to eat and starves to death in a few weeks. This behavior shows that chimpanzees can feel emotions as strongly as humans do.

◈◈ CHIMPANZEE COMMUNITIES ◈◈

Chimpanzees live in groups called communities. Each community has fifteen to eighty members, but most have around fifty individuals. A community's **home range** varies from 2 to 20 square miles (5 to 52 sq km) in forests and 45 to 215 square miles (117 to 557 sq km) in grassland areas. Males stay in the same community all their lives, but females often join other communities when they become adults.

Male chimpanzees guard their home range. Chimpanzees do not fight often, but scientists have seen one community start a "war" with another community.

Chimpanzee communities split up into small groups every morning to look for food. This group is sharing a banana.

Each morning, the members of a community break up into small groups of two to eight chimpanzees. These groups, usually made up of a mother and her children or friends, hunt for food together. If they find a huge tree loaded with fruit, they inform the whole community with loud screams and cries.

A young chimpanzee will stay near its mother its whole life. A mother chimpanzee has a very special bond with her children.

34

Each community has one ***alpha male***—a male who is the "big boss." This male always has the first choice of food and first rights to mate with females. The alpha male is not always the largest chimpanzee in the community, but he is the most aggressive—and often the smartest. A chimpanzee can become the alpha male by challenging other chimpanzees with yells and threats. Occasionally, a chimpanzee may fight to become the alpha male.

Lower in rank than the alpha male are less powerful "little bosses." The power structure among the little bosses changes often. In most communities, female chimpanzees rank even lower than the male little bosses.

When female chimpanzees reach 13 years of age, they begin to mate with the males in their community. Females are pregnant for 8 months and generally have one 4-pound (1.8-kg) baby every 5 years. Babies are usually cared for by their mother, but if a mother chimpanzee dies, other adults may take care of her children.

A baby chimpanzee is born helpless and clings to its mother's stomach for about 5 months. Then it rides on its mother's back and soon starts to walk and climb. Although a baby chimpanzee drinks mother's milk for about 5 years, it starts growing teeth and eating solid food at 3 to 5 months of age. A young chimpanzee stays close to its mother all its life. A mother chimpanzee and her children have a very special bond.

As a chimpanzee grows older, its black hair turns gray and thins out, just like a human's hair. Older chimpanzees are respected by the younger members of their community.

◈ A DAY IN THE LIFE ◈

All wild chimpanzees live in West and Central Africa, north of the Zaire River. They live in lush rain forests and in sparse forests. Each day, they wake up slowly, groom each other, and then begin to search for food.

Are you a fussy eater? Chimpanzees aren't. They eat more than 300 types of fruits, stems, and nuts as well as insects. Sometimes they hunt young bush pigs, baby red colobus monkeys, young bushbucks, bird eggs, and chicks. They occasionally kill and eat baby chimpanzees from other communities.

Chimpanzees are the only great apes that hunt in groups. They may take several hours to chase and finally catch a monkey before devouring it. The alpha male usually leads the hunt.

After eating for 2 or 3 hours, chimpanzees rest, play, swing hand over hand through the trees, and spend time with each other. Later in the day they look for food again. Although chimpanzees are more skilled than gorillas at walking on two legs, they spend most of their time on all fours. They may cover up to 4 miles (6.4 km) a day searching for food.

Chimpanzees spend a lot of time grooming each other, and always stay near friends and family.

Chimpanzees spend a lot of time in the trees. Each night, they weave sleeping nests in the trees with sticks and leaves. Young children sleep in the same nest as their mothers.

Although chimpanzees often live for more than 50 years, they face many dangers. They are hunted by lions, leopards, and, sometimes, baboons. A tree branch may break and bring a chimpanzee crashing to the ground. Chimpanzees may also catch human diseases like polio and colds. When they are sick, chimpanzees sometimes eat leaves with medicinal healing properties!

◈ BONOBOS AND CHIMPANZEES ◈

Even though bonobos look a lot like common chimpanzees, they are different enough to be considered a separate species. Bonobos live only in central Zaire, south of the Zaire River. Because they are smaller than common chimpanzees, they are sometimes called pygmy, or dwarf, chimpanzees.

Bonobos are more slender and graceful than chimpanzees, and they spend more time in the trees. While the arms of common chimpanzees are noticeably longer than their legs, the arms of bonobos are about the same length as their legs. Bonobos have smaller ears, smaller heads, and darker faces than chimpanzees. The hair on the top of their heads is parted down the center, and they look like they have sideburns. They also have red lips. Like chimpanzees, bonobos have good hearing, vision, and sense of smell and taste. Their feet and hands are prehensile, so they can grip branches and tools.

Bonobos are slightly smaller than chimpanzees. But they are just as smart as, more gentle than, and more closely related to humans than chimpanzees.

A large male bonobo is very strong—much stronger than a human!

Bonobos have closer-knit communities than common chimpanzees, and females play a more dominant role. Bonobos do not kill their young and seem much less aggressive and violent than common chimpanzees toward each other and toward other communities. They are at least as smart as chimpanzees and are thought to be slightly more closely related to humans than chimpanzees are.

When male orangutans inflate their throat sack, they can give an earsplitting "long call."

4
Orangutans

A large male orangutan sits quietly in a tree, near a female. Suddenly it hears a smaller male orangutan approaching through the forest. The large orangutan inflates the throat sack under its chin like a big balloon and gives out an earsplitting "long call." This series of deafening groans and roars lasts about 4 minutesand can be heard more than 1 mile (1.6 km) away. Then the large orangutan shakes a tree branch and pushes over a dead tree that crashes to the ground! The smaller orangutan is scared and quickly leaves the area.

Male orangutans sometimes fight each other to mate with females, but most of the time they try to avoid each other. In fact, orangutans are actually gentle, shy animals that spend most of their time alone.

◈◦◈ ORANGUTAN SOCIETY ◈◦◈

Why do orangutans spend more time alone than any other great ape? It probably has something to do with their diet. Orangutans eat a lot of food, especially fruit. And, since fruit is spread all over the forest, orangutans would have a hard time getting enough to eat if they traveled in large groups.

Baby orangutans stay with their mothers for 4 to 5 years. Then the male youngsters move to a home range far away from their mothers. The young females move to a home range that overlaps their mother's home range. Adult female orangutans have home ranges that overlap with those of adult male orangutans.

An adult female orangutan spends a great deal of time with its children, so females are not alone as much as males. The female may also travel for a few days or weeks with other females or its older children. Occasionally, young males travel together for short periods. Young males always avoid adult males.

◈◦◈ ORANGUTAN FAMILIES ◈◦◈

Female orangutans start to mate when they are about 12 years old. They have four or five babies during their

Like chimpanzees, female orangutans raise their young without the assistance of males. This mother and her youngster will spend all of their time together until the baby is 4 or 5 years old.

A baby orangutan clings to its mother's back until it is strong enough to climb on its own.

lifetime—one baby every 8 or 9 years. Females mate with the biggest, strongest males they can find. About 8 ½ months after mating, they give birth to a 2- to 3-pound (1- to 1.4-kg) baby.

Like all great apes, the baby orangutan is born helpless and clings to its mother's stomach until it is strong enough to ride on its mother's back. By the time a baby is 1 year old, it weighs about 15 pounds (6.8 kg) and eats some solid food. It drinks its mother's milk for about 4 years, then it begins to climb more and eat large quantities of solid food.

When the mother is ready to mate again, it forces the youngster out of the nest. A male youngster will still stay near the mother for a while, but gradually moves away. However, a female youngster stays with the mother as much as a year longer. By watching the mother raise a new baby, the young female learns how to take care of the young she will one day have. Eventually, the young female moves to a nearby area.

How often do orangutans have family reunions? Hardly ever! The males never return, except to mate. Brothers and sisters rarely see each other, and daughters see their mothers only occasionally.

✥ DAILY LIFE FOR AN ORANGUTAN ✥

Like all great apes, orangutans build sleeping nests in the trees at night. In just a few minutes they weave branches together into a comfortable nest. Sometimes they build a leafy roof over their nest to shelter them from wind and rain. Large male orangutans often build their nests on the ground.

Orangutans spend most of their time in the trees.

Each morning, mother orangutans groom their offspring before they begin their 100- to 900-yard (91- to 822-m) journey in search of food. Every once in a while, the orangutans stop and take naps in daytime nests. They often sit in the trees for hours and do nothing at all.

Baby orangutans usually play with their mothers or by themselves, because other babies are not around. They swing, climb, and hang upside down. When they do meet other youngsters, they wrestle, chase each other, and do somersaults.

These animals spend most of their time in trees, 70 to 130 feet (20 to 40 m) above the ground. Adult females and their young rarely come down to the forest floor, except to eat termites. Large males walk on the ground while looking for food and then climb into the trees to eat it.

On the ground, adult orangutans move very slowly and deliberately. But they can move through the trees faster than people can move through the thick forest beneath them. Orangutans like water and will sometimes wade up to their hips across jungle streams.

❖ HABITAT AND FOOD ❖

Orangutans, the only great apes in Asia, are the world's largest tree-dwelling, or *arboreal*, animals. They live in the rain forests of two islands, Borneo and Sumatra. Sumatra tigers and leopards sometimes attack baby orangutans, but adult orangutans have no natural enemies.

These apes eat more than 400 types of fruit, including lychees, figs, mangoes, and sweet plums. When fruit is not available, they munch on leaves, ferns, flowers, and even birds' eggs. They also love termites and honey. Orangutans have even been seen eating baby birds and squirrels. They get the water they need by licking it off leaves or scooping it out of tree holes with their hands.

Male orangutans live in home ranges of 2 to 3 square miles (5 to 8 sq km). They sometimes become nomadic, traveling over large areas to find food. Females have smaller home ranges, and usually do not leave them. Younger males and females without home ranges are nomadic.

This young orangutan is enjoying a meal of fruit.

Adult male orangutans have wide cheek pads, beards, a throat pouch, and long canine teeth. They use these features to intimidate enemies.

◈ ORANGUTAN BODIES ◈

In the Malaysian language, *orangutan* means "person of the forest." They are also called red apes. There are two subspecies of orangutans. Sumatran orangutans have mostly orange hair, and the males have oval faces. Borneo orangutans have mostly brown hair, and the males have round faces.

Orangutan males reach adulthood at 12 to 15 years old, and females are adults at 7 to 10. These animals may live to be 50 or 60 years old. As they get older, their hair grows darker.

Adult males are 4.5 feet (1.4 m) tall, can weigh more than 200 pounds (90 kg), and are five times stronger than humans! They have beards, wide cheek pads, throat pouches, large canine teeth, and long flowing hair. Adult females stand up to 3.5 feet (1.1 m) tall and weigh up to 110 pounds (50 kg). They don't have cheek flaps, beards, or throat pouches.

When they are on the ground, orangutans walk on all fours, applying most of their weight to the outsides of their feet and their cupped hands. Their powerful arms may span up to 8 feet (2.5 m), but their legs are much shorter and weaker. That's why is easier for orangutans to swing through the trees than to walk on the ground.

Orangutans use their powerful jaws to rip open tough fruit shells. They have good eyesight and hearing as well as highly developed senses of smell and taste. Their feet and hands are prehensile, so they can grab branches with both.

❖ INTELLIGENCE AND EMOTIONS ❖

Like other great apes, orangutans have a wide range of emotions. They are also very smart, and a few have been taught sign language. They make many sounds—

Some orangutans have been seen using tools to catch termites, just like chimpanzees.

grunts, barks, squeaks, and screams—and often use body language to communicate.

Captive orangutans use tools at least as well as chimpanzees. Some wild orangutans use sticks to eat termites, ants, fruit, and honey—and to scratch their backs. When it rains, they hold leaves over their heads like umbrellas. These animals have excellent memories. This is an important trait because they need to remember when hundreds of types of trees will have ripe fruit. If they forget when trees bear fruit, they might go hungry!

Jane Goodall was the first female scientist to study chimpanzees. She proved that they have emotions, intelligence, and complicated communities.

5

Efforts to Save the Great Apes

Who made the great apes famous? Jane Goodall studied chimpanzees, Dian Fossey studied gorillas, and Biruté Galdikas studied orangutans.

During the 1960s, Louis S. B. Leakey, a famous *anthropologist,* asked all three women to study the great apes, and helped them get started. Leakey believed women would be more open to observing the humanlike qualities of great apes. At that time, many scientists refused to believe that other animals have emotions or are intelligent. Goodall, Fossey, and Galdikas showed these scientists that they were wrong.

Unfortunately, even as the world learned more about great apes, many

55

Many great apes are still being killed illegally for souvenirs, for food, and for folk medicines.

were being captured and sold to zoos, circuses, and pet stores. Others were sold to laboratories for medical research. Still others were killed for food or so that their heads and hands could be sold as souvenirs. At the same time, loggers were cutting down the rain forests where the great apes lived. Because many of these problems still exist today, all great apes are in danger of *extinction*.

However, efforts are being made to save these wonderful animals. Many of their habitats have been made into national parks and sanctuaries. The trees in these areas cannot be cut down, and the animals living

GREAT APE POPULATIONS IN THE WILD

GREAT APE	ESTIMATED POPULATION	LOCATION OF PARKS AND SANCTUARIES
GORILLA	600 to 110,000*	Cameroon, Central African Republic, Congo, Gabon, Rwanda, Uganda, Zaire
COMMON CHIMPANZEE	105,000 to 175,000	Cameroon, Congo, Nigeria, Tanzania, Uganda
BONOBO	10,000 to 20,000	Zaire
ORANGUTAN	17,000 to 29,000	Borneo, Sumatra

*There are about 600 mountain gorillas, 10,000 eastern lowland gorillas, and more than 110,000 western lowland gorillas.

there cannot be hunted. Some countries are welcoming *ecotourists*—vacationers who pay to see great apes and other wildlife in their natural settings. The money spent by these travelers is used to support local economies as well as to protect wildlife and its habitat.

People who live near rain forests are learning that if the forests are destroyed, the soil will not grow crops. People are also being taught to use rain forest products to help support themselves. In other programs, young great apes that are orphaned or found as illegal pets are being *rehabilitated*. They are taught how to live in the rain forests and then released into the wild. These programs have had mixed success.

Dian Fossey proved that gorillas are smart, shy, and gentle creatures. She died trying to protect them from poachers.

An international agreement known as the Convention in International Trade in Endangered Species in Wild Fauna and Flora (CITES) is also working to control—or stop—global wildlife trade.

Despite all these efforts, the ***poaching*** continues, even in protected wildlife parks. Many countries do not have enough money to protect their parks. When times are difficult, local people often turn to great apes for food or souvenirs.

What is the future of the great apes? It depends on human beings. We have the power to destroy them or save them. It is up to us.

 glossary

alpha male—the dominant "big boss" male among chimpanzees.

altitude—an expression of height above sea level.

anthropologist—a scientist who studies humans and their origins.

arboreal—an animal that lives in trees.

body language— facial and body gestures used to communicate.

ecotourist—a vacationer who pays to see wildlife in its natural setting.

evolve—develop or change over a long period of time, adapting to current living conditions.

extinction—the dying out of a species.

habitat—the area in which an animal normally lives and grows.

home range—the area in which an animal spends most of its time and life.

hominid—a group of primates that includes all humans and their direct ancestors.

nomadic—roaming over a large area and not living in any one place.

offspring—the babies or young of an organism.

poaching—killing animals illegally.

polygamous—having more than one mate.

predator—an animal that survives by eating another animal.

prehensile—a hand or foot with the big toe or thumb opposite the other toes or fingers. This allows an animal to seize, grab, or wrap its hand or foot around objects.

primate—a group of mammals that includes apes, monkeys, and humans.

rain forest—a forest with a yearly rainfall of at least 100 inches (254 cm).

rehabilitate—restore to a former state of health or ability.

sign language—hand signals used to communicate.

silverback—the dominant male in a gorilla troop.

species—a group of animals that look alike and can reproduce only with each other.

stereoscopic—vision that allows the observer to see depth; or to see in three dimensions.

subspecies—a subdivision of a species. Different subspecies usually look slightly different and live in different geographic areas, but can mate and produce young with each other.

trait—an inherited quality or characteristic.

troop—a small group of animals.

resources

BOOKS

Gallardo, Evelyn. *Among the Orangutans: The Biruté Galdikas Story*. San Francisco: Chronicle Books, 1993.

Goodall, Jane. *The Chimpanzee Family Book*. Saxonville: Picture Book Studio, 1989.

Patterson, Francine. *Koko's Kitten*. New York: Scholastic, 1985.

ORGANIZATIONS

The Jane Goodall Institute
P.O. Box 599
Ridgefield, CT 06877
TEL: (203) 431-2099
FAX: (203) 431-4387
**http://www.wcsu.
ctstateu.edu/
cyberchimp/**

The Gorilla Foundation
Box 620-640
Woodside, CA 94062
TEL: (415) 851-8505
FAX: (415) 851-0291
http://www.gorilla.org

**Orangutan Foundation
International**
822 S. Wellesley Ave.
Los Angeles, CA 90049
TEL: (310) 207-1655
FAX: (310) 207-1556
**http://www.ns.net/
orangutan**

Attn: Gorilla Conservation
Campaign
**Wildlife Conservation
Society**
185th St. & Southern Blvd.
Bronx, NY 10460
TEL: (718) 220-7159
FAX: (718) 364-4275
http://www.wcs.org

index

Geoffrey C. Saign loves to sail, dive on reefs, and hike in forests. He has a background in wildlife biology and has assisted in field research on a number of animals including hummingbirds and humpback whales. *The Great Apes* is Mr. Saign's first book for Franklin Watts. He is also the author of the nationally endorsed *Green Essentials: What You Need to Know About the Environment* (Mercury House, 1994). Mr. Saign has also spent a decade counseling disadvantaged children and adolescents. He currently lives in St. Paul, Minnesota.